Chasing the sunlight

A survivor's assessment of decomposition (Zersetzung) methods as employed in 21st Century Britain and Ireland

By Joe Bloggs

Chasing the sunlight: A survivor's assessment of decomposition (Zersetzung) methods as employed in 21st Century Britain and Ireland

Table of contents

Introduction

Chapter 1

Chapter 2

General assessment of decomposition methods:

Appendix

'May the Lord bless and keep you'

(A Christian blessing inspired by The Holy Bible,
numbers 6:24 KJV)

Introduction

I begin this book with the hope that it brings light to the abhorrent practice of decomposition, or Zersetzung as it is known in German. Briefly stated, decomposition is the application of various influences and pressures to people so that their mental, emotional, or physical health deteriorates. This is done so that in conjunction with these effects they are either slowed down in their endeavours or are, in effect, paralysed. Historically, it involved the equivalent of prolonged group based gaslighting and the unproven but suspected use of directed-energy weapons. In the modern day, it involves more advanced versions of both of these, as well as the manipulation of online digital screen-based technology in order to negatively affect the user. I hope to expose to the general public what decomposition is and how it is currently applied.

I can say with certainty that it is practiced in the modern day in both England and Ireland. I know because I have been on the receiving end of it for at least 12 years and I think in all likelihood up to 20 years. As of 2022, I am 39 years old. My life has been in tatters for many years and I have been more or less paralysed in terms of the work which I have been able to achieve. I know I am not invincible. My mental health, like my physical health, can only withstand so much abuse. Fortuitously, the situation has arisen whereby I have the time, energy, and knowledge with which to recount what my experiences have been. In addition, I can contextualise my personal account in regard to the historiography of the practice, which is most explicitly emphasised by the history of socialist East Germany. There are numerous other examples both historical and modern. I am not alone in suffering this extreme form of silent repression and hidden abuse. There are, and have been, many victims. I believe that I have been targeted with such methods due to my writing which includes theories in philosophy and physics. There may be other reasons related to politics and finance for example, but these are more ambiguous in terms of whether they provide enough motivation for intense and prolonged decomposition methods to be applied. Although I would say, with humility, that a potential to be successful in these fields is likely a contributary factor to why I have been targeted in the way that I have been.

…

Update: After about six and a half months of working on this book I have made slow progress. The above statements are the first half of the original introduction.

I have found it difficult to work properly due to the decomposition methods currently being applied to myself. For this reason, I have chosen not to wait until the book is more finished but instead publish a short version now as a 1st edition. I have included a draft introduction to the originally intended fuller version in the appendix. This will give you an idea of what to expect in the 2nd edition. I ask for your forbearance with this and for you to understand that this is a live situation. I am under huge pressure and I struggle to perform day to day tasks, and writing is also difficult. In this edition I have considered decomposition methods in general. I have based it nearly entirely on my own experiences. However, it is not based solely on my experiences. A few examples have been assumed to possibly occur based upon my knowledge of how decomposition methods work in general. In this book, such theoretical examples serve the purpose of better explaining the greater theory which they relate to. The literature I have read about decomposition I do not directly refer to in this edition, with the exception of its relatively brief mention in the appendix. It seems fair to say, though, that it has been an influence on my reasoning to some extent, even if sub-consciously.

I have used my experiences to try to form an interpretation of decomposition methods and their intended effects. A critical voice on this may immediately say that I should not use a single person's experiences, even my own, as evidence for how a large-scale system of repression which is, presumably, targeted at a substantial number of people operates. I recognise this concern but I ask for people to understand that I am also struggling to make sense of the nature of what has and indeed continues to be happening. It is difficult. And understanding what has been targeted at me in terms of a system which is designed to be targeted at anyone seems to help. Perhaps it is an act of distancing what has happened from myself which helps, or an act of perspective-based empathy with the decomposers in order to better understand their intentions which helps. Whatever the answer, for now these are the only reasonably complete sections of the book which I can go ahead with. By the time you have read this short book, you should have a good general idea of what decomposition methods involve in the modern day and the effects that they have on a person.

I have written under a pseudonym.

Brief overview of decomposition methods

What is decomposition and why is it used?

Decomposition is a group based control method designed to damage people to the point of inactivity and socially isolate them. It does this by causing such pressures, stresses, and harms that the person, or group, becomes effectively paralysed and has very limited functionality. Ordinarily, people and groups are targeted because they are considered to be a threat in some manner, or will potentially become one in the future. In terms of what threat they represent, this could be considered as being something which may challenge the ambitions of the organisation carrying out the decomposition methods, or their employers. Decomposition methods are usually carried out by state intelligence or security services, operating domestically or abroad, and ancillary groups i.e. domestic collaborators in a given country. Decomposition methods are best known to have been conducted for political and cultural reasons i.e. as a means of repressing politically incorrect people without physically arresting them. Among the main contributary reasons that people were targeted historically was due to a perceived ability to influence others, or to have the potential to develop such an ability in the future; and for promoting politically incorrect views or thought processes, or be potentially going to promote them in the future. For example, religious groups, writers, artists, youth sub-culture groups, is to name a few 'types' of people who have been targeted. Decomposition methods can be applied covertly, so the target is not aware of them, and overtly so the target is aware of them. I will discuss this in more detail later on.

In terms of the historical and modern record, decomposition methods are closely associated with socialist (or communist) governments, faux socialist governments, and post-socialist countries. But their practice should not be thought of as being limited to adherents of these ideological, governmental and national identities, or for reasons solely related to popularity and political incorrectness. They have been widely used globally for many reasons, including to gain advantage in business and technological development i.e. attempting to render someone incapable of protesting effectively about the theft of their ideas or product.

Decomposition methods are standardly employed in a group based manner. For example, a large group of people will typically manage the decomposition of a single person. As most decomposition methods seem to be conducted by state aligned agencies it can be assumed that the available resources for decomposition methods in these cases are defined by the agencies resources, plus any collaborators i.e. Israel's Mossad plus domestic Sayanim (volunteers). How the resources for decomposition are gathered, allocated and applied in practice in the modern day is hard to say. In terms of the application of decomposition methods, geographically considered, there is definitely a willingness and ability to track people from location to location, including internationally. Aside from the reason of maintaining the repression of the victim, it also means that they will be less likely to become aware of the method being formerly applied by way of contrast with its current absence i.e. if the repression is suddenly removed because the person moves, then they will realise something has changed and be much more likely to identify retrospectively that something was affecting them negatively, and even realise that it was form of targeted silent repression.

Are decomposition methods openly applied or are they secretly applied?

Ordinarily, they are meant to be applied secretly so that the target is not aware of them. Overall, this effectiveness is reduced when the target is aware of them and can mitigate against their effects. Also, if the target has witnesses it becomes much more difficult to frame them as being paranoid and delusional, and of making insane accusations. Whether actualised or not, the threat of this kind of fit up is immense and causes people to self-isolate and remain silent. It should be remembered that even in the ostensibly free countries of the Western world, involuntary commitment to a mental asylum is never based on a jury trial, but can be implemented on the basis of an agreement between two or so psychiatrists who perceive poor mental health and possible violent intention. Many modern states have gained themselves the ability to incarcerate people against their will without the hard fought for safeguard of judgement by non-affiliated people from the general public being present.

There are several ways that the threat of incarceration in this manner can be considered in regard to decomposition methods. One possibility is that the person is not aware of the decomposition methods being applied but as they are causing psychological damage, they perceive an increased threat to their mental health and of being incarcerated in an asylum. This threat is lessened if the decomposition methods are known about: as the person can identify the cause they know they are not losing their mind. In addition, if there are witnesses, it becomes much harder to frame the person as insane. However, if the person is aware that they are being targeted then this is extremely intimidating. It also allows for gaslighting techniques to become really powerful as the person attempts to identify what everyday happenings are not in fact everyday, and whether people who they know, or meet, are not in fact who and what they present themselves as. In other words, they can reduce a person's sense of security across the board and lead to them questioning everything.

For most people, if decomposition methods are applied too forcefully then they will become aware that they are being targeted. Sooner or later they will become conscious of the methods. So the question for the people carrying out the decomposition is: keep it low level and hard to detect, or make it intense, run the risk of being detected, but be able to apply a lot more repressive force? The latter of these examples relies on the fact that people find it very hard to talk about these things going on because they are afraid that to do so runs the risk of a straight jacket. The application of overt (to the target, not to witnesses which would be massively counter-productive) decomposition methods relies on relatively unaccountable mental health legislation and the unethical and unjust state powers of prolonged incarceration and drugging, in order to intimidate the target into silence. Certainly maintaining silence due to a fear of this was the case with myself.

Brief overview of decomposition methods

Historically, decomposition of a target individual or group was primarily based upon various forms of gaslighting, false representation and impersonation of typological identity, and various forms of intimidation. It should be noted that threats made could be actualised- they were not empty threats.

In the modern day, decomposition methods have three main branches. They are group based gaslighting, directed-energy weapons, and electronic screen manipulation.

Gaslighting (psychological harassment)

Gaslighting is a relatively well-known term which roughly means attempting to cause someone to doubt their sense of reality, or something similar. In this common definition, a person or small group are usually considered to attempt to gaslight a single person who is socially isolated or becomes so. The term is used to refer to any action undertaken which may cause the targeted person to doubt their sense of reality. Such actions are ordinarily undertaken with the intention of causing some kind of permanent mental health damage to the target.

The usefulness of the expression in regard to decomposition methods, is that decomposition methods have a similar intention of undermining a person's sanity by manipulating their social relationships and physical environment. The similarities are so striking in this regard that decomposition methods of this type can be said to be synonymous with or involve gaslighting methods. That is why I have chosen to use the term here, and also because it is a relatively well-known term, it allows for an understanding of what decomposition methods can involve to be more quickly established. The main point of difference is that decomposition methods are undertaken by a large, well organised group with all the additional practical capabilities which that implies.

It should be noted that when decomposition methods are referred to in academic and journalistic sources, they are only sometimes referred to as gaslighting. They may also be referred to as psychological warfare, psychological harassment and so forth. For the rest of this book, gaslighting will be meant solely in regard to how it exists as an integral part of decomposition methods, unless otherwise stated.

Directed-energy weapons

Directed-energy weapons, abbreviated as DEWs, are manufactured or improvised devices which propagate directed-energy (DE) so as to in some way harm or cause distress to people. Here, I refer to those which propagate electro-magnetic radiation, or sound beams usually in the ultrasonic part of the spectrum. Many DEWs have a range of several miles and can penetrate buildings with limited attenuation.

Electronic screen manipulation

This is something I am less certain on. The main reason is that many of the debilitative effects I suffered, which were potentially caused by this, I suffered whilst also being targeted with directed energy. So it is hard to clearly identify what caused the effects. This is the theory on electronic screen manipulation (ESM) as I currently have it: that the screen refresh rate, colours, brightness, contrast, zoom, and other details can be altered in a negative way by the software installed on the hardware. For example, on a Windows PC the operating system can influence the refresh rate, colour, brightness etc. The idea is that a hacker with bad intentions, or a virus, can manipulate these settings so that they change frequently. The repeated alteration, which may conform to a pattern or be an irregular series of changes, can cause negative effects on the user, or other physiological responses. This would be by influencing the action of the eye which can also have a knock-on effect on the function of the brain in general and a person's cognition. So, for example, in my experience I could use my PC for a period of time, say for 30 minutes to a couple of hours, before getting off with very sore eyes and a splitting headache. I would lie on my bed until the pain subsided. I should add that when I was using the computer I was in a state which was reminiscent of being hypnotised and just mindlessly clicking along. You may think that these are relatively common symptoms produced by too much screen time, but I impress upon you that if they are similar in nature that my experiences have been an extreme version of it. Partly for these reasons of inducing prolonged and compulsive use, whilst concurrently causing pain to the eyes and brain, and a feeling of nausea, I suspect that there is the potential for the screen properties to be caused to fluctuate in a negative manner. I have had similar experiences when using my laptop in public spaces and far from my house. Considered in contrast, this effect does not occur when using other people's hardware: most notably public computers such as those found in a library, or university desktops or laptops. The negative effects simply do not occur to anything near a similar extent.

Gaslighting

Specific forms

Home intrusion

This is where people enter the targets residence illegally without them having prior awareness that the event would take place. This may be done to achieve several things. For example, theft of personal possessions in order to reduce the target's ability to operate. To leave signs of some sort such as a new object, or to move an object already present in the residence. Such forms of home intrusion carry with them the threat not only that the person's objects can be manipulated but they, as a person, can be accessed. This can mean that their home, which should be a place of safety, becomes a place of fear, especially if they live alone. Whereas physical seclusion may have brought with it comfort in the sense of safety, it now amplifies the perceived threat of physical harm as it means that there will be no witnesses to help them. Fears related to this can be immense and can extend to

16

that of prolonged, direct physical torture and death. As with other forms of decomposition methods which challenge the security of the home, they may be, depending on the intention, counter-poised with methods which encourage the person to stay living in that location. The person is therefore strongly motivated by two different imperatives: one to seek safety at their home, and the other to leave their home to seek safety. Moving home is the obvious way to improve the situation, and for this reason decomposition methods are designed to ensure that the target is, where possible, kept at a level of financial poverty, and does not have the ability to move home or live elsewhere.

As with other forms of decomposition, home intrusion may work better against some targets than others. For this reason decomposition methods are tailored for each individual, and are used as part of a set of methods and not in isolation.

Altered social actions and positionings

This essentially means people doing things in such a manner that you believe that they may have a specific relevance to you which is not being openly stated or directly declared. This may involve them performing an action so as to imply that they are signalling a message to you or about you, are observing you or your family and friends, threatening you etc.

For example, someone being by the roadside on the phone and looking constantly at you as you drove past. It is worth noting that, unless paranoid, you believe it may have a relevance to you, and may is the operative word. You believe it may have a relevance because of either it is genuinely unusual behaviour in its own right, or preceding events help to construct a general context where you believe such interpretations are more plausible. In the latter example, one way in which this can work is that the incidents considered individually may not be considered unusual enough to warrant any particular attention. However, considered collectively their unusual natures are amplified in the mind of the target, and so any of them considered individually are more likely to be interpreted by the target as being some form of contrived social construct indirectly targeted at them.

Considered in terms of its thematic relevance, such an incident also acts as a prompt for you to consider that you are being followed and observed in general. The formerly stated example is also a form of pre-emptive marking or following i.e. the person doing the marking or following predicts where the person will be and waits for them there. The target may, on this basis, think it is taking a risk to plan things as this can therefore allow them to be pre-empted in their movements by the decomposers. The target may come to the conclusion that it is safer to do things with as limited prior notice as possible, or to keep any plans they make as secret as possible. This will ordinarily mean that their ability to plan, and thereby act in an efficient manner, is significantly reduced.

The messages given, range in terms of their complexity and impact. A more complex example is where a family member is mimicked in some way in order to demonstrate their sustained close surveillance. Thematically, this again prompts the target to consider that they themselves are being observed but this time with the added consideration of it being long-term, intensive, and can involve their replacement: an act which necessarily means their removal in some manner either by abduction or death. The fact that the observation can be performed to that extent, serves as evidence to the target that their abduction or murder are achievable for the decomposers. Such a deduction being made by the target can dramatically increase the sense of threat they feel. Threatening a person's family or friends due to their association with them may also mean that they are loathe to make new friends or keep in touch with old friends as it may put them in danger. Again, this demonstrates the ability of decomposition methods to isolate people.

Symptoms and effects

Confusion

Causing confusion is the fundamental aim of gaslighting. When a person becomes confused they are less able to plan and make decisions effectively. Their capacity to work in a meaningful way is therefore reduced. As their confusion becomes more regular they also become anxious.

A person may become confused about: their physical security or that of those they care about; thresholds and accesses considered in physical terms of whether they should be in or are welcome in a particular location, or this same consideration based in regard to other people; identities and loyalties in terms of who's who and who can be trusted; etiquettes and social skills in terms of what appropriate behaviour is for themselves or for others.

Anxiety

A person who has become increasingly unsure of how to interpret the world around them will begin to feel increasingly anxious. So gaslighting which causes confusion will also cause anxiety.

Another way in which gaslighting can cause anxiety is by indirect physical intimidation which is delivered in a manner which is identifiable but hard to be entirely sure of, and very difficult to challenge as it is so difficult to prove. An example would be an allusion to a violent act which was not directed at you, but stated or performed in such a manner that you would witness it. You therefore receive the impression that this could be directed at you, and this coupled with the fact that you cannot prove it and therefore feel you cannot challenge it, can cause anxiety. Indeed, it can cause very intense anxiety depending on how far you think the threat extends and whether you think there is a realistic chance of it being carried out. The possibility of a punch in the face is a worry, but the prospect of abduction and prolonged, direct physical torture is terrifying. It is worth noting that anxiety and threats can work sub-consciously. Even if not being particularly considered on an active basis, the knowledge that they exist can bring about a tendency in people to avoid doing anything which they think may bring the threat to be actualised. On this basis, if a person thought it was their work which the decomposers wanted to suppress, then they would become less inclined to carry on with that work, even if they never consciously decided this as such.

Paranoia

Paranoia results from the confusion and the anxiety. Essentially the target cannot make sense of things correctly and moves along a path of mental progression whereby they increasingly make judgements which are false and anxiety producing. It can be a vicious cycle with the person becoming increasingly paranoid. This is not to say though that they are necessarily wrong in all of their judgements or that there is not an element of justification to their paranoia. The point I make here is that they are over-assuming things, making an increasing number of mistakes, and their judgement overall is becoming increasingly inaccurate and negative on this basis. For example, they may start from quite reasonably not trusting one person, to ending up not trusting anyone i.e. they are all out to get me.

As the person becomes increasingly paranoid, they may be accused of making paranoid claims and of constructing a paranoid narrative of fictional events. This puts them in a position whereby their word will be doubted, in terms of the value of the work which they have produced, creative or research based, and in terms of their account of what events have taken place. In terms of covert decomposition methods, the target is therefore much less able to prove that they are being targeted as there is less of an obvious reason for the targeting because their work is perceived of less value.

It may also mean that they are less likely to be given credit for their work, in any instance, as people believe that they make false claims in general and therefore may be falsifying its originality. This may mean two things: firstly, that it is easier for their work to be stolen as they find it harder to prove it is theirs; and secondly, they are again less likely to be believed in regard to claiming they are being targeted as their work has been stolen and credited to somebody else, there is less of an apparent reason which would explain why they would be targeted in the first place. As the person is portrayed publicly as making things up in terms of what has happened, it makes their work much easier to steal.

Distraction

Decomposition methods, including gaslighting, may be frequently or constantly applied to a person. This may mean a greater or lesser workload depending on the intensity of the application. Dealing with the effects of gaslighting methods can be extremely time consuming and energy sapping. In such cases, a person will struggle to achieve other forms of work.

In addition, the nature of the gaslighting methods may mean that a person's attention is directed away from a particular piece of work and towards something else i.e. distracted away from a politically incorrect, religiously incorrect or in some other way undesirable project which the decomposers consider counter-productive to their attempts to influence the public, and towards whether anyone has illegal access to their property.

They may also be distracted from a desirable project they are working on so as to make it easier to steal. The work can then be further developed by the decomposer or their employer. This makes it easier for them to claim that the work in its entirety is theirs, as they have developed it to an extent. Necessarily, it also makes it easier to claim that any protests made by the person who begun the work, the targeted person, are fraudulent. And there may be many others reasons that the decomposers seek to stop the target from working by way of distraction.

Fatigue

Dealing with the effects of gaslighting on a sustained basis is exhausting. A person may be thinking and working overtime trying to understand what is happening and what its significance is. This may be the case even when no gaslighting is actually taking place because the person does not know that. All they know is that there has been a series of incidents which have either caused them to doubt their rationality or sanity, or that they find suspicious i.e. they understand someone is involved in manufacturing some or all of the confusing incidents, which based upon their suspected orchestration also become threatening. In forms of gaslighting delivered covertly, when the targeted person does not suspect anyone else is involved, they will be attempting to form rational, secure judgments and work through an idea they have formed that they are beginning to fail to understand things. This in itself can take considerable time and effort and is probably a more difficult situation to be in than when it is understood that the incidents are orchestrated. Whether the gaslighting is part of an overt or covert decomposition strategy, a person's expectancy of another event occurring, which they have to deal with, means that they may try to prepare to excess and forget to take due rest i.e. they will be continually thinking about what happened, can they challenge it safely, what is going to happen next etc. Such a lack of rest heightens their fatigue.

When a person is fatigued they are more prone to becoming confused and anxious. There can be a vicious cycle formed between these factors, with each leading to an increase in the other. In terms of the practical implementation of gaslighting as a decomposition method, it may only be necessary to start the person off and then top them up every so often. In other words, the gaslighting is introduced so as to elicit an intense questioning thought cycle by the target. This process would ordinarily come to a natural stop over a period of time when the person could not identify any more troubling incidents. So it is necessary to introduce new gaslighting incidents in order that the person reasonably expects that they will continue to experience them and have to deal with them. But overall, the gaslighting incidents implemented may be relatively small; the person, however, may expect, quite reasonably, that it is an ongoing issue that they will have to deal with and, mistakenly but understandably, overcommit in terms of the time and effort they spend trying to understand what is happening. This can lead to fatigue and associated effects.

It is also worth noting that the stress from the gaslighting can cause poor digestion. This can mean the person is, in effect, going hungry and this can also lead to an increase in fatigue. Similarly, it can cause a reduction in sleep quality and increase fatigue in that manner.

Directed-energy weapons

The specific forms of energy weapon are varied and ordinarily not identifiable directly. I am confident that they include sound-based energy, and electro-magnetic radiation (EMR), presumably microwaves. Some of their effects can be mitigated against somewhat by the use of earplugs and earthing methods, both during the day and at night. The intensity of the DEWs can be increased to make such measures relatively meaningless, in terms of stopping a person being effectively debilitated. However, the measures may mean that a less preferential form of DEW based repression has to be applied i.e. they need to use a different form of microwave pulse than they would have otherwise. Another possibility is that the effectiveness of the ear plugs and earthing is essentially allowed so as to give the target the impression that they can cope with what is going on and are able to exert some kind of influence on the situation.

Whatever the case in terms of mitigation measures, it seems highly likely that the DEWs include sound and EMR. This can be deduced via the symptoms they produce and the effects they have. On this basis, I will describe some of the symptoms and effects which can be produced.

Symptoms and effects

Vibrations on the skin

A vibrating feeling on the skin, especially on the face and upper torso. Most commonly felt in bed but can also be felt when entering an area targeted by DEWs.

There may also be a much slower tapping sensation felt on the skin soon after waking. This occurs in conjunction with a feeling like you have been physically beaten during the night.

Pulsed shocks

These are single pulses which cause a sudden movement of the body. This movement can feel like a pulsed shock, a kind of muscle spasm, or being suddenly pushed as if by an invisible force. The range of power varies considerably. Examples include:

*Small pulsed shocks which occur in or around the spine of the neck.

*A powerful shock which causes a very violent jerk of the head and makes it feel like your neck might break, and could be broken at will by the decomposers.

*A feeling like being pushed suddenly and forcefully into the bed before bouncing back up again. This push commonly feels like energy hitting the shoulder before quickly spreading and dissipating.

Throbbing teeth

A feeling like energy pulsing through your teeth and them throbbing and chattering as a result.

Paralysis

DEWs can cause someone to wake up in a partial or whole state or paralysis. This lasts for a short period of time, not more than 5 minutes. When it is partial it is often the case that movement of the head and neck is retained.

Muscle sprains and joint aches

Muscle sprains, including of the lower back, can be precipitated by DEWs in a short period of time without prior aggravating factors.

Joints can also be caused to feel very tight and contracted which can lead to injury.

Interference with thought or mood.

The DEWs interfere with the normal process of cognition so a person find it is difficult to think. This may mean that they find it difficult to consider that different possibilities exist, to think in depth, to converse normally, take on board new information, remember things, appreciate the significance of things etc. In addition, a person may also be caused to feel tense, afraid, giddy, over-excited, frustrated, sexually aroused etc.

Mind blanking

This relates to influencing a person's memory so that they barely remember something and it loses its significance to them. This may even be the case for long-held ambitions and things which have been committed to. A person's future intentions can be manipulated in this way.

Amplification of alcohol

This is where the DEWs are used to amplify the addictive qualities of alcohol, and enhance its damaging effect.

In terms of addiction, this relates to inhibiting the body's ability to process the alcohol so that its intoxicating effect is amplified. Crucially, it stays in the person's system longer meaning that the person is intoxicated for longer periods.

In terms of damage, considered in the short-term, this primarily relates to amplification of a hangover. Nausea, vomiting and headaches can be dramatically increased in terms of the intensity of their effect. This may be done to the point of severe levels of pain and distress.

Even small quantities of alcohol can be made to be debilitative in this regard. While the effects will not be as severe, they can still cause a hangover to occur due to the body's inability to process the alcohol properly.

An alternative explanation of this situation, is that the DEWs cause the same symptoms of a hangover and use the alcohol as a masking factor. Whilst it is an unrealistic masking factor in small quantities, it allows for plausible deniability in regard to the involvement of another factor such as a DEW. For example, if the target was to say to a lay person, 'I have not drunk enough to warrant a hangover but I have been assaulted with directed-energy weapons and this has caused the symptoms', it is unlikely they would be believed. And, again, it would put them in a situation where mental health legislation may be brought to bear against them.

DEWs can also be applied in a manner so that when a person is not drinking alcohol, the DEW is turned on, which produces a negative physiological response such as a feeling of depression, and when they are drinking, it is turned off. Thus, drinking alcohol is relatively encouraged.

Deafness

The causing of deafness in one or both ears, either wholly or partially. In terms of how each ear is affected, the levels of deafness may be fluctuated i.e. the left ear nearly wholly deafened, and the right ear slightly deafened. The deafness may be temporary or permanent. An ongoing alternation between the causing of temporary deafness, and allowed partial recovery, may be enacted in such a way that the person becomes gradually permanently deafened, whilst getting the impression in the short term, that their hearing is recovering. If such an implementation is combined with forms of distraction, and cognitive impairment relating to thought and memory, then this can reduce the likelihood of the person identifying what is happening, or of reacting in such a way that improves their situation.

Methods used include the use of acoustic hailing devices (AHDs), which can generate powerful, and thin, beams of directed sound, to cause increasingly high-pitched tones in the ear; and to cause the sound of metal sheets being crushed and crumpled together and scraping on each-other, to be heard on either the periphery of human hearing or subliminally. For example, the person is aware that this is a loud noise that they have been hearing during sleep but they were not aware of consciously hearing it at the time, not did it wake anyone else in the vicinity. Two things could explain this, either considered individually or in conjunction: the hearing of the sound was caused by a sound beam so as to isolate the hearing of the sound to the target; and the hearing of it was related somehow to the hysteresis effect, which is whereby you can hear a sound at a lower amplitude when you are continuing to hear it, and it is reducing to a point that you cannot hear it anymore. This is considered in comparison to when it is increasing in amplitude and whereby it has to be relatively louder for you to be able to begin to hear it.

Deafness, including partial and tone deafness, cannot just limit someone's employment opportunities but also their ability to socialise properly, as being able to understand and convey tone correctly is an essential part of being able to converse in an engaging and charismatic manner.

Alteration of appearance

DEWs can be used to cause a negative alteration of a person's appearance. Standardly, this is a by-product of their use to achieve other goals. For example, if the DEWs are used to cause exhaustion and chronic fatigue, then these symptoms will cause a person to look de-energised, run down, and generally unwell. This makes them less socially appealing and also less sexually attractive. These things make it harder for the person to progress socially and romantically, and may increase their isolation.

Sensation of waves

DEWs may also cause the sensation of waves passing through the head and body. It is relatively uncommon. They can give the sensation of a wave, considered as a series of smaller waves, of movement, or a wave of vibration, passing through the head or body. They are more likely to be felt through the head than the body, and in such cases they can usually be felt to extend through it in its entirety, or thereabouts. In regard to the body, it is more usual for them to be felt as the vibrations on the skin, extending somewhat into it and the underlying flesh and muscle.

Both typically occur in conjunction with a general state of exhaustion and chronic fatigue. They immediately give rise to the fear of cancer or other disease being caused by repeated exposure. A fear which persists for at least as long as the targeting does.

Intense directed force

DEWs can be used to cause intense feelings of force in the body, such as being stabbed by something i.e. an acute driving pain which penetrates a part of the body, such as the abdomen.

Immediate exhaustion

DEWs, employed in a very intense manner, can cause the person to very quickly stop what they are doing due to an uncomfortable feeling of utter exhaustion, which also causes them to leave the area. When they do so, their energy levels normalise.

The pairing and separation of mental and physical exhaustion

If it is considered that a person's mind and body are parts of a greater whole, then both can be exhausted by DEWs together, or one can be targeted and the other not. The mind is targeted by the brain being targeted directly. The body is targeted in various ways including by the heart being targeted directly. If both are targeted then this is as a means of debilitating the person so as to cause them to be house bound or inclined to find a quiet place to recuperate and not engage socially.

When the brain is targeted and not the body, this can be used to allow the person to have the energy to go out, but to do so in a manner which is less mentally fit and well than it would be otherwise. As such, they may socialise but come across to people as being mentally impaired, in some way, to some extent. It may also allow them to feel confident enough to undertake physical tasks but not have the required mental ability to do so successfully; this can dramatically increase the chance of them injuring themselves.

It should be noted that the mind and body, being linked so closely, cannot be targeted in complete isolation of each other. When one is targeted the other will also suffer, although not to the same extent. The impairment of what is targeted is greater and is therefore more emphasised, causing the hitherto stated effects.

Heart beat and breathing rate

The target's heart rate and breathing rate can be influenced by the DEWs. Other factors such as depth and force can also be influenced. This can be achieved by targeting the heart or breathing system directly, or by other methods, including influencing their action through the use of sound which is heard and targeting the crown of the head.

The influence of the DEWs may result in an excessively high and irregular heartbeat. In terms of breathing, they may be used to stall breathing, cause sleep apnea, or excessively shallow breathing.

Among other things, these changes can be used to encourage negative changes in mood, energy levels, cognitive ability and memory.

Other forms of targeting.

The crown of the head is frequently targeted by DEWs. This is for the reason that its impairment or relative paralysis has the general effect of debilitating the person because it has a direct effect on all mental and physical processes. In addition, if the target is taller than other people in a location, the DEW beams can be set to hit and irradiate their crown whilst going over the heads of everybody else.

Images, which look like pictures, can be caused to appear in the eyes and in the front part of the head. In terms of the former, flashing images with each flash meaning a new image. In the case of the latter, six pictures arranged in squares with three in the top row and three in the bottom. There are at least two explanations: that the DEW beam contained the images in some way, and this is what the person sees as they reach the appropriate part of the optical or mental anatomy. Or alternatively, that the seeing of the pictures is a physiological response, involving the imagining of the pictures, due to the stimulation of this part of their anatomy by the DEWs i.e. they imagine the pictures as this is one way in which their brain copes with the irradiation.

Directionality

It is very difficult to ascertain the direction the directed-energy is coming from. This is the case even when there appears to be a clear sensation of lineal and focused irradiation along a vector. This interpretation is made because it would mean that, in some circumstances, that the DEW had to be very small and hidable, and have a hidden power supply, and the decomposers willing to take a very significant risk of it being found. It is possible but unlikely given the alternative of using a longer range untraceable DEW which could achieve a similar debilitative effect by using a higher power setting.

Another consideration which arises from the question of the target's perception, or not, of which direction the directed-energy is coming from, is whether it can be applied in such a way that suggests it comes from a direction it does not in fact come from. This could be used to encourage the person to look for the DEW, not find anything, and then be in a situation of needing to explain their search to witnesses of it. A statement that they had been targeted by a DEW and were looking for it may make them look paranoid, even delusional, and again run the risk of incarceration under mental health legislation.

It is worth considering that decomposers take great pains to never be found out and to isolate any individual aware that they are being targeted from potentially supportive witnesses. On this basis, it is highly likely that there is a very powerful sweeper system in place to deal with any potential fallout which may occur if they are caught. A move from covert decomposition methods to overt decomposition methods may be the result of the activation of this sweeper system.

Fatigue

DEWs can cause exhaustion immediately. However, in terms of causing long-term states of fatigue, this is generally precipitated by repeated exposure over a prolonged period i.e. targeting someone during sleep in their home. Fatigue standardly means a person will have prolonged low energy levels, and this reduces their capability to work and achieve things across the board. In a way, it reduces a person's life as they are not just less capable but they move slower in general and need more rest. All of which reduce their ability to work and socialise.

Intimidation

Being shot by an energy weapon is intimidating in its own right, but coupled with the facts that a person will ordinarily be being shot from unknown locations, that the DE passes through walls and windows, that it is extremely difficult to locate the firing positions, and it becomes obvious how they can be used to terrorise people. They again build on the psychological theme that there are no safe spaces, and you can be accessed wherever you go.

Disease

DEWs can cause disease based upon repeated exposure. The greater the exposure, the greater the risk. Those which use ionising radiation, such as X-rays, presumably can achieve this effect more quickly.

Reduction of mental ability

DEWs can cause a reduction of mental ability in the short and long term. This can involve traumatic brain injuries.

Influence of social relationships

DEWs may be used to debilitate a target so that they find it more difficult to socialise. For example, a reduction in energy levels, cognitive ability, memory, and emotional and nervous capacity, can make socialising successfully difficult and its attempt very stressful.

The people who socialise with the target can also be targeted when they are together, or have recently socialised together. As long as the interaction with the target is directly associated with the negative effects of the directed-energy, then socialising with the target may be considered as being the cause of the negative effects. This relies on the people targeted being unaware that a DEW was causing the negative effects, and the effects should be of a kind that could reasonably come from a social interaction i.e. feeling uncomfortable, stressed, anxious, bored etc.

Influencing social relationships in such ways is intended to socially isolate the target, and make such isolation look either self-inflicted or based upon social rejection. It should be noted that DEWs may have extensive range up to several miles or more, significant penetrative capabilities, and that any major Western urban area will likely have some form of DEW network set up. Coupled with smart phone tracking using GPS, it is possible for a person to be targeted extensively, if not fully, in such areas- this includes when they are inside buildings.

Indoctrination

To impress upon the person certain viewpoints and processes of judgement. This is done, presumably, through the subliminal perception of sound, verbal statements or otherwise, which is projected from an acoustic hailing device.

Such indoctrination may additionally involve the concurrent stimulation of physiological responses such as that of the brain, including the crown of the head, nervous system, heart, and respiratory system. The intention being to pair the projected sound message with the physiological response i.e. the idea of employment paired with a stressful contraction of the nervous system; or the idea of carrying out work in a particular field with the relative deactivation of the brain (considered in terms of the processes of cognition which would ordinarily be involved in such a task).

Acute emotional distress

Put simply, being targeted with DEWs is a form of torture. It will usually have various permutations and intensities to its application but nearly always it is emotionally distressing to a greater or lesser extent. This means that the person targeted will find it more difficult to work in any regard. The intensity of the DEW, considered in isolation or on the basis of cumulative effect* is never intended to be so weak that it provides a stimulus for positive action in excess of its debilitative effects. Such a thing would be obviously counter-productive in regard to the purpose of decomposition methods. The person will also find it harder to do other things such as socialising. The emotional difficulties caused may even culminate in them feeling unable to leave the house. They are therefore much more likely to isolate themselves, thus fulfilling one of the key ambitions of the decomposers.

*This is related to a person's threshold for tolerance. Roughly speaking, assuming the exposure to the DE is increased in excess of the person's ability to recover, then each additional unit of DE will have an increasingly damaging effect as the person becomes increasingly wounded. This can also relate to their being overloaded with pain, or some other negative feeling, and therefore feeling additional pain, even if only slight, that much more acutely. I suppose this could be considered in percentage terms. If a person has one hundred percent capacity to cope with pain, as this capacity gets filled then each additional unit of pain has a greater and greater significance, as it represents a proportional increase relative to the remaining capacity to cope with it. A bit like when someone who is long-term ill can have a very low pain threshold even though they may, by apparent contrast, exhibit extraordinary strength of mind to be able to keep going. It is worth noting that many of the effects caused by decomposition do make a person, in effect, behave as if they have a long-term illness of some type. Ultimately, if the decomposition methods do cause disease then this can be used to retrospectively explain the person's previous fatigue and inability to work. On a related point, and I am by no means an expert on this, but I think that the intimidating aspects of decomposition, considered in terms of their effect on a person's psychology, may also be found in

cases of severe domestic abuse. Certainly there
appears to be some common elements.

Electronic screen manipulation

As with DEWs, an assessment of electronic screen manipulation (ESM) is based primarily on the symptoms produced. However, as ESM is standardly employed in conjunction with DEWs, there is a question as to what symptoms are caused by what method, and even a question as to whether ESM exists. In theory, ESM relies on the fluctuation of an aspect or aspects of the screen's formation. Electronic screen in this case meaning one which is connected to some form of computer processing system which is connected to the internet. So the theory appertains to desktops, laptops, and smartphones. It is plausible that ESM software may be installed onto a device when it is connected online and continue to function on it when it is offline.

The screen's formation and its respective manipulation may involve the fluctuation of its brightness, contrast, resolution, size, zoom percentage, or some other factor. These may be caused to alter in a regular pattern or irregularly. The type of content displayed on the screen may be associated with a particular pattern, or lack thereof, through its occurrence in tandem with it over a period of time. This would also associate the content with the symptom and effects caused by the pattern.

Some of the symptoms of ESM are similar to those encountered when using unmanipulated electronic devices and their respective screens. If it is considered that the screen refresh rate is a form of intense oscillation and can produce symptoms such as sore eyes, mental fatigue, and minor hypnotic effects, then a person may think that the symptoms of ESM theory are not anything out of the ordinary and thereby disprove its existence. However, even if the symptoms of ESM are similar in type to those which can be produced by unmanipulated electronic-screens, it should be realised that they are much more powerful, fast acting, and long lasting. The symptoms produced by ESM can be very obvious.

Symptoms and effects

Sore eyes

The eyes become sore during use. This continues for some time after the device has been used. It produces the desire to shut them tightly as a form of relief. Or to gently massage them with the fingers or a cool damp cloth.

Headache

This occurs during use and becomes increasingly painful. The pain continues after use. It can produce the desire to hold the head as a form of relief. The headache can also involve a feeling of tightness and pain in the forehead area.

Nausea

A feeling of nausea during use which gets increasingly worse and continues for a period after use.

Induced repetitive action

This is whereby the person is compelled to use the device and look at the screen for prolonged periods, despite the negative effects building up i.e. despite the headache, nausea, and sore eyes.

Typically this effect will also occur in tandem with reduced cognition and memory. As such, the continued use of the device is not limited by the person realising how long they have spent doing so i.e. the person's state of mind is caused to fluctuate in various ways so they consider it as one long period of time, less. They become increasingly concerned with their immediate use of the device, in relative isolation from their remembered use of the device over the last seconds, minutes or hours. In addition, a form of tunnel vision can be initiated with the person's focus becoming increasingly dominated by their engagement with the device and the screen, and less on any other mental consideration.

These things combined may be said to elicit a form of compulsive use, although stopping short of full hypnosis or trance.

Impaired cognition

Electronic screen manipulation can cause an impairment of the person's ability to think and reason properly. Their consideration of what to do in terms of how they use the device can become increasingly immediate and based upon visual stimuli and less on planned action i.e. they become easily led or distracted from what they intended to do by the content of the screen. As their mind becomes increasingly preoccupied with coping with the negative effects of the ESM, and this may be considered to be an instinctive protective response performed on a sub-conscious basis, their ability to think normally and rationally is reduced. Thoughts, ideas and memories which may ordinarily occur to them, are much less likely to occur and this makes their conscious decision making process much more based upon immediate stimuli, such as the electronic screen.

Impaired memory

This relates primarily to the person's use of their memory whilst the ESM is occurring, and their ability to form new memories during. Both are reduced. The person will remember things outside of the immediate visual stimuli less than usual, perhaps very significantly so, and they will be less likely to be able to remember what they have been doing whilst under the effects of the ESM. This results in the person being increasingly influenced by the content of the screen, without being able to assess the consequences of their actions, by process of memory, as effectively.

Difficulty seeing and being able to read

The ESM can mean the person's ability to see clearly is reduced. This may mean that they have difficulty reading writing on the screen. It should be noted that impaired cognition and memory caused by the ESM can also mean that reading comprehension is dramatically reduced. It may be the case that a person cannot make sense of a single line of simple text. The causing of this symptom can make research and writing very difficult.

Mood

ESM can influence mood in various ways including encouraging anxiety, frustration, giddiness, and sexual arousal. For example, a sense of anxiety can be encouraged based upon a person looking at photos of people on a website for jobs they are going to apply for. The causing of the anxiety concurrently with their viewing of the people dissuades them from applying for the job, and also makes them afraid, to an extent, of people in general. Another example, is that a person may be caused to feel giddy during their use of the device, and this may cause them to wander around the room in a giddy, dazed state of mind.

Stunned

A person may be stunned by the ESM meaning that they are less conscious of what they are doing, think less rationally, and remember things less. Their overall energy levels will also be reduced. Their posture may be poor and fixed for long periods of time, even hours, without changing.

Fatigue

ESM drains a person's energy both mentally and physically, rendering them less able to work in any respect.

Reduced cognition and impaired memory (after effects)

This not only involves the reduction of these during the use of the devices, but continues for a period after. The recovery rate is relatively fast but can last a few hours and extend up to several days depending on the intensity and duration of exposure. Considered separately from effects related to deliberate indoctrination, to what extent behaviour and user habits are altered by prolonged exposure to ESM is unclear. Similarly, the extent of the influence on eyesight over the long-term is unknown.

Time wasting

ESM produces substantial periods of time wasting and procrastination. It has the added advantage of it looking self-inflicted because it clearly is the user who is controlling the device. The fact that the user behaviour is being influenced is hidden. One way to think of this is that the user's time wasting activities on the device are a forced error as opposed to an unforced error. It is also worth noting that decomposition methods can be highly distressing for various reasons; when they are reduced because the target is wasting their time in a manner which looks self-inflicted, it is a comforting experience for the target because it offers a reprieve. From the decomposer's perspective, assuming they are at this stage interested in achieving a relatively light version of decomposition, then it is a positive situation. The target is not doing anything of particular worth, they are wasting their time, and indeed life, and to witnesses it appears to be self-inflicted. In the case of the latter, a witness may also think that the victim lacks character, is a low-person for not trying to do more positive things, and as the case may be, letting other people take the strain of any necessary work load. This means that another decomposition target, that of discrediting a person, is also achieved.

Indoctrination

To alter someone's perspective of and reaction to various things. This is based in regard to the content of the screen and is typically in regard to a type of thing. This is for the reason that it is easier to pair a psychological or physiological response with the viewing of a type of thing (which tends to be relatively higher frequency viewing) than the viewing of a single example of that type (which would ordinarily tend to be a lower frequency viewing). Although in the latter case it is still possible, although the person would have to have a reason to repeatedly view that single thing.

Over a period of time, the repeated stimulation of the psychological or physiological response in concurrency with such a viewing on the screen, forms a psychological association in the mind of the person. They expect each of the pair to occur when the other does. This in turn influences how they appreciate and understand the content, and their respective attitude towards it. In this manner, a person can be indoctrinated to think particular ways about different things, which can usually be identified based upon the type of thing that they are.

Integration (with each other and with day to day events in the person's life)

Decomposition methods are standardly employed in a manner where the different branches of method are integrated into the same system of silent repression. Where possible, gaslighting will be combined with directed-energy weapons, and one or both will be combined with electronic screen manipulation. These three categories do not account for every method used which may contribute to the repression. There is a willingness to use any and all options available.

There may be considered to be two forms of integration: dependent integration, whereby one or more decomposition methods are dependent on each other to be successful. And bulk integration whereby the methods are used together to increase the overall force or impact of the methods, but this could have been achieved by a single method given the appropriate resources. For example, the use of gaslighting and directed-energy weapons to produce anxiety. Either one of them could have produced higher levels independently but both were used either due to a lack of available resources for any one method or simply as a way of spreading the workload. Such methods may be powerful and potentially break down the target quicker but may not be particularly tailored and lack finesse. They may also be easier to identify as they may lack an ability to mask themselves as effectively using the person's personal circumstances.

To return to a discussion of dependent integration, as stated, this is where one or more methods of integration is dependent on the other to work successfully. Generally, this may mean it amplifies its effect or masks it. For example, waking someone during the night with a pulse of directed-energy may both amplify the stressful effects, meant in the illness inducing sense, of the gaslighting while also distracting attention away from them as being a cause of the stress.

Another example would be a person becoming paranoid, apparently by the effects of the gaslighting in and of itself, but actually the application of directed-energy to them during their sleep has caused substantial strain to their central nervous system making the gaslighting extremely hard to cope with on a mental and emotional level. In this example, the gaslighting itself would not have been enough to elicit this effect although it is considered to be the cause. Paranoid thought processes can also be instigated or amplified by AHDs or similar subliminal measures. This can be of fundamental importance in the target interpreting the slightly unusual events as involved in the gaslighting and as being of hostile underlying intent; they may just shrug otherwise and put it down to random chance or similar. So the AHD allows for the gaslighting effect to be amplified, and the gaslighting acts as a masking factor for the application of the AHD.

Once in a paranoid state of mind, a person may interpret normal everyday events, and not manipulated ones, as being unusual or threatening in some manner. At this stage, there is no longer any need to continue to introduce manipulated events or gaslight the target. Their current mindset is such that they will perceive things in a paranoid manner anyway; this can be continued, and the person not allowed to regain normal mental equilibrium, through the use of directed-energy weapons. Decomposition methods can also be integrated with unmanipulated events which a person may go through. For example, bereavement and DEWs. The grief can be amplified and the person unable to recover emotionally. The bereavement is used as camouflage for the implementation of the DEWs, which disrupts the normal healing process whilst causing symptoms which, to an observer, appear to be prolonged grief. In this way the person's emotional health is being continuously manipulated by the decomposers whilst making the bereavement appear to be the causal factor.

Decomposition methods may be, and frequently are, integrated with everyday events and activities. One standard example is the integration of DEWs and ESM with electronic devices. The method involves the variation of DEWs and ESM, based upon what the person is looking at, or more generally construed, the type of thing they are looking at. For example, they are looking at things related to gaining employment: the DEWs, ESM, or both, are caused to have a negative effect on the person. The person therefore associates that endeavour (in this case, seeking to improve their situation in life which would also mean counteracting or limiting the negative effects of the decomposition) with the negative experience from the DEWs or ESM. Conversely, the DEWs and ESM may be removed or turned off when the person is doing something which they are not meant to be doing i.e. procrastinating or wasting their time surfing the net and looking at random media. The person therefore associates this misspending of their time with a sense of relief and feeling more themselves. Alternatively, the DEW or ESM may be used to elicit a sensation which is positive in some way i.e. pleasurable, in connection with them doing something which is negative in some regard. In addition to promoting actions which may be considered negative, and dissuading actions which may be considered as being positive, these methods can also be used in an attempt to channel and indoctrinate a person towards having a particular psychology, learnt physiological responses based upon typologically orientated stimulus, and conducting particular actions; or vice versa.

Other forms of integration include DEWs with social interactions. For example, a person interacts with another person. A DEW is then applied to the area negatively affecting them both. Each person associates the negative effect, which causes them to feel bad, with the other person. They may think that the other person is the cause or that interacting with them is the cause. They make think that there is something wrong with them. This will make it less likely that they will meet up again or remain in contact. Or a DEW with a larger area of effect can be targeted at a person when they are in a public area and make them seem dislikeable to the public who are around. Such effects can enhance the isolating effect of the decomposition methods. A similar effect of manipulating people's perception, can be achieved in regard to the application of a directed-energy weapon to an area or building, which thereby dissuades, its use; or by the removal of the DE, relatively encourages its use.

Gaslighting, in general, should be considered as always being integrated into everyday events, necessarily. This is because it needs to be in order to create the impression of ambiguity which it so heavily relies on. For example, if a person is home alone and a pen which they have not seen before, of the free giveaway variety, is placed upon the desk which they have just recently been working at, without them knowing how it got there or recognising it, they are presented with several possibilities: that the pen was placed by someone who had illegally entered their home as a form of threat or message; or that they picked up the pen and put it there themselves without remembering, after all these things happen all the time. So the two possibilities exist as extremes to each other and both are based on the innocuous presence of a cheap, promotional pen. To speak about something so seemingly everyday and harmless as if it represented an extreme threat i.e. hostile persons being able to physically access them at will while they were in their home, would immediately put them at risk of sounding paranoid and potentially insane. Is it possible to go to the police with such a complaint? Is it worth the risk of falling foul of mental health legislation? Such an example demonstrates how it is the integration of the decomposition method with the everyday that allows it to both carry its threat value, remain hidden to all but the target, and to put them in a state of confusion, anxiety and indecision.

The likelihood of the target interpreting the unusual event as being some form of purposeful manipulation, related to a threatening or non-threatening communication, can be increased. This can be done either through the way the event is set in relation to the target, or timing the event to be in correspondence with something which will increase the susceptibility of the person to interpret it as being orchestrated communication of some kind. In terms of initial gaslighting events, these may be compared with sales hooks designed to hook a prospective customer into a sales funnel where sales methods can be consistently applied to them. Only in this case the person is encouraged to continuously identify the covert manipulation of the everyday. Plausibly, there may also be conditioning methods integrated into the person's life prior to the beginning of the gaslighting in order to encourage them to view the unusual events as being orchestrated; such conditioning may be integrated months or years before the gaslighting. For example, encouraging a person to believe that people have undeclared ulterior motives, that there are hidden networks etc. Both things which are undeniably true to some extent; as part of a pre-conditioning programme the aim is to encourage the person to over-emphasise their likelihood so as to make them more prone to make an interpretation that someone is trying to gaslight them. This relates to the style of gaslighting used in overt decomposition methods and not covert decomposition methods. Which would suggest that the decomposers can predict for which targets they are more likely to need to apply the greater level of repression that overt decomposition methods allow for.

Appendix

A brief analysis of other writers' interpretations of decomposition methods

In this section I will briefly analyse some quotes which demonstrate how decomposition methods have been employed in socialist East Germany at the end of the 20th Century, and in modern Russia at the start of the 21st Century. The purpose is to demonstrate that the claims made in the main body of the work do not exist in isolation: the practice is known about even if consciousness of it is not yet mainstream. A great many people have been targeted.

Stasiland is a book which contains multiple accounts from people who lived in East Germany under socialist rule. It includes accounts from the general public and people who worked for the Stasi. In the notes section in the back of the book, it gives a description of decomposition methods:

> I later found instructions to operatives on ways of crippling 'oppositional' people, which gave more detail than Herr Bock's little lecture. It comes from the Directive 'Perceptions'

(Richtlinen, Stichpunkt Wahrnehmung'). It aims:
To develop apathy (in the subject)... to achieve
a situation in which his conflicts, whether of a
social, personal, career, health or political kind
are irresolvable... to give rise to fears in him... to
develop/create disappointments... to restrict his
talents or capabilities... to reduce his capacity to
act and... to harness dissentions and
contradictions around him for that purpose...[1]

The above quote demonstrates how a person could be
targeted for being 'oppositional'. Such people could
come from all walks of life and be targeted for various
reasons. That decomposition methods could be directed
at such a range of people shows how versatile a method
it is.

The journalist Luke Harding was targeted by
decomposition methods, circa 2007, in Russia. In an
attempt to understand his targeting he researched
Zersetzung and attained various interviews. He states
that:

---

[1] Funder, Anna, 'Some Notes on Sources' in *Stasiland*,
London: Granta Books, 2004, pp. 285-286

'The most insidious aspect of *Zersetzung* is that its victims are invariably not believed. When Frau R told her friends what was happening they concluded that she was losing touch with reality: 'We found it impossible to explain why someone would want to remove the hand towels,' one of them admitted. Some *Zersetzung* victims think they are going mad or are ill, those affected suffer the reproach that they are hallucinating.'[2]

The above quote relates to a victim's experience in East Germany under the Stasi. It highlights how a small, relatively inconspicuous alteration to someone's property within their home, via illegal entry, can put someone in a situation where they are accused of hallucinating and fear that they are 'going mad'. Not only does this carry the threat of potential incarceration and drugging under mental health legislation, but it can also isolate someone from their support network just by their discussion of the events. While Harding does not directly mention the sense of physical threat that someone having ready access to your home can bring, he does so later on in regard to his own experiences of people entering his residence in Russia: 'The intruders' aim seems merely to demonstrate that they had been

---

[2] Harding, Luke, *Mafia State*, London: Guardian Faber Publishing, 2007, p.284

there- and to show, presumably, that they can come back, if the mood takes them. [...] The dark symbolism of the open window in the children's bedroom is not hard to decipher: take care, or your kids might just fall out.'[3] Harding's experience demonstrates the intertwining of gaslighting with physical threat, and the conveying of the idea to the target that the decomposers can access them at will. He considers this in regard to how such methods were developed by the Stasi: 'These methods of intimidation and anonymous harassment were classified as 'operational psychology'. Operational psychology is conventional psychology's dark twin: instead of healing people, the idea is to harm or damage them.'[4] The terms intimidation and anonymous harassment do not properly do justice to the sense of fear that the methods can generate. This statement does, however, succinctly sum up one of the main goals of decomposition methods: to harm or damage a person.

According to the historian Mike Dennis in his work, *The Stasi: Myth and Reality*:

> 'The decomposition methods referred to earlier were an essential ingredient of OVs (operational cases) and, according to the 1976 guidelines, were to be 'applied, extended and further developed in a creative and differentiated

---

[3] Harding, pp.284-285
[4] Harding, pp.284-285

manner according to the 'concrete conditions' of each case. An OV was terminated either when proof of a crime was obtained or if an offence could be prevented. In the harsh language of a 1985 regulation relating to a central operational case, the criteria for termination included 'undermining, paralysing or rendering harmless the hostile forces in such a way that they only carry out their hostile activities at a low level of intensity and danger to society or they are not capable of any acute subversive activity so that they can be dealt with or controlled by different methods.'[5]

Using Stasi records as his source, Dennis highlights how people were targeted in a tailored fashion and that the overarching intention was 'undermining, paralysing or rendering harmless the hostiles forces'. There are a number of points which can be considered here. I will start in reverse order. The hostile forces could be anyone who the Stasi deemed appropriate for cultural, religious or political reasons. It demonstrates that, as a method, decomposition can be applied flexibly, to different people who are selected based upon the decomposers reasoning of what a hostile person is. This means it cannot just be targeted at writers or church members etc., but it can also be targeted at business

---

[5] Dennis, Mike, *The Stasi: Myth and Reality*, London: Routledge, 2003, p.114

people, street sweepers, or any individual or group who is deemed hostile based upon the perspective of the people undertaking the decomposition. It is, in this manner, a highly transferable way of breaking down anybody who is deemed an appropriate target. The fact that decomposition methods can be tailored based upon the psychology and lifestyle of the individuals' targeted, allows this to be the case. However, on this subject, the historians Jens Giesehe and David Burnett state that for the Stasi, 'It was possible, at any rate, to run a certain 'standard program' without much effort and effectively make rebellious citizens preoccupied with themselves, e.g., by refusing to provide them with adequate work or spreading slanderous rumours.'[6] While it is unlikely that these were the only methods of silent repression applied to such citizens, it suggests that it was only necessary to begin the silent repression and at intervals of some distance apart reinforce it; this is meant in regard to their continued or recurrent awareness that they are being targeted, which precipitates an ongoing attempt to try to understand and, indeed, re-understand the circumstances of their lives in order to regain a sense of security, both mentally and physically. This destabilising effect can be disorientating and extremely powerful. If one person copes better with it than others, then the intensity and

---

[6] Giesehe, Jens & Burnett, David, *The History of the Stasi: East Germany's Secret Police 1945-1990*, 2015, p.151

duration of the methods can always be increased for them. Causing financial hardship through limiting of the target's ability to work is notably also mentioned. This generally means social isolation, and the various stresses and problems which come with limited finances or poverty.

In an extensive study, the historian Andreas Glaesar, details from Stasi sources the purpose of decomposition methods:

> 'Proven methods of decomposition to be used are:
>
> Systematic destruction of public reputation, standing, and prestige on the basis of the connection between true, verifiable, and discrediting as well as untrue, credible, non-disprovable, and thus equally discrediting information;
>
> Systematic organisation of professional and social failures to undermine the self-confidence of individual persons;
>
> [...]

Busying groups, groupings, and organizations with their own internal problems with the goal to limit their inimical-negative actions'[7]

The first point demonstrates how the methods are designed to discredit people in various ways and thereby socially isolate them. The second focuses on how a person's life can be destroyed in various ways. Again, the descriptions concise and technical form does not accurately convey the extreme and destructive effect that non-stop professional and social failure has on a person's life. Self-confidence is of fundamental importance to a person being able to progress successfully and to be able to overcome repression, and this is no doubt why it receives specific mention in the Stasi's list of things to focus on damaging. The third point shows how the target of decomposition is continuously distracted from carry on the activities which the decomposition methods are being utilised to prevent. Giesehe and Burnett also state that one of the intentions of decomposition methods was to divert 'attention to secondary areas of conflict.'[8] This further demonstrates that not only could debilitation methods designed to restrict a target's ability to operate be used, but various methods of distraction could be employed

---

[7] Glaesar, Andreas, *Political Epistemics: The Secret Police, The Opposition, and the End of East German Socialism*, 2010, Chicago: University of Chicago, pp.495-496
[8] Giesehe & Burnett, p.151

in conjunction in order to further neutralise the perceived problem presented by the target's activity.

David Hoffman, focuses his study on how decomposition methods were 'brought to the streets of Havana.'[9] Whilst, in combination with East Germany and modern Russia, this may suggest a connection to countries with communist associations, it would be a mistake to think that they are unique to this ideology. Luke Harding states, 'According to Girke (Jochen Girke, former chair of operational Psychology at the Stasi's higher academy), all secret services, including Western ones, use what he calls 'grubby tools'.'[10] This is meant in regard to decomposition methods. Whatever the truth of the claim, I think that decomposition methods are used a lot more widely than the public is aware of. Indeed, I think it is reasonable to suggest that where the repressive forces of political correctness are particularly strong, or there is a market in the theft of intellectual property, or even just a lot of money to be made, that decomposition methods may be found to be employed, to a greater or lesser extent.

primarily decomposition methods are used by rich and powerful groups, state aligned or not, to repress relatively poor and powerless people either for reasons

---

[9] Hoffman, David E., *Give me Liberty: The True Story of Oswaldo Payá and his Daring Quest for a Free Cuba*, New York: Simon Schuster, p.224

[10] Harding, p.287

of social engineering, prevention of terrorism (perhaps the only justifiable reason), and to ensure successful acts of theft whilst limiting fallout.

In his PhD thesis, Ulrike L. Neuendorf, states that 'Various authors, in particular psychiatrists and psychologists, have discussed how the *Zersetzung* method had devastating and long-lasting effects on peoples' lives, breaking apart families and friendships and leaving victims with severe psychological damage. Authors include Peters 1991; Seidler & Froese 2006; Bomberg & Trobisch-Lütge 2009; Trobisch-Lütge 2010; Priebe et al. 1996 and Freyberger et al. 2003.'[11] I mention this last just to show that there is a slowly increasing field of research into how decomposition methods have been employed. It is nice to think that soon its modern application may be brought into mainstream public consciousness and this may help to secure the freedom of the innocent.

---

[11] Neuendorf, Ulrike L., *Surveillance and Control: An Ethnographic Study of the Legacy of the Stasi and its impact on wellbeing,* London: University College London, 2016/2017, pp.228-229

Introduction (original draft)

I begin this book with the hope that it brings light to the abhorrent practice of decomposition, or Zersetzung as it is known in German. Briefly stated, decomposition is the application of various influences and pressures to people so that their mental, emotional, or physical health deteriorates. This is done so that in conjunction with these effects they are either slowed down in their endeavours or are, in effect, paralysed. Historically, it involved the equivalent of prolonged group based gaslighting and the unproven but suspected use of directed-energy weapons. In the modern day, it involves more advanced versions of both of these, as well as the manipulation of online digital screen-based technology in order to negatively affect the user. I hope to expose to the general public what decomposition is, what it was, and how it is currently applied.

I can say with certainty that it is practiced in the modern day in both England and Ireland. I know because I have been on the receiving end of it for at least 12 years and I think in all likelihood up to 20 years. As of 2022, I am 39 years old. My life has been in tatters for many years and I have been more or less paralysed in terms of the work which I have been able to achieve. I know I am not invincible. My mental health, like my physical health, can only withstand so much abuse. Fortuitously, the situation has arisen whereby I have the time, energy, and knowledge with which to recount what my experiences have been. In addition, I can contextualise my personal account in regard to the historiography of the practice, which is most explicitly emphasised by the history of socialist East Germany. There are numerous other examples both historical and modern. I am not alone in suffering this extreme form of silent repression and hidden abuse. There are, and have been, many victims.

In this book I will firstly explain what decomposition is in greater detail. I will then discuss it in regard to its history. After this I will discuss reports of its application in the modern day. These things are important as they allow for the identification of decomposition methods in the context of a field of general study and research. In addition to improving the comprehension and understanding of people unused to hearing about such forms of repression, it also means that other survivors and I can speak about what has happened, or is happening, to us without the fear of talking as isolated individuals and thereby running the very real risk of being condemned via mental health legislation as being paranoid and delusional-charges which could lead to involuntary commitment and the associated coerced or forced taking of powerful drugs. And as with any study or research, more examples analysed generally means more accurate and intelligible findings.

After giving this background information, I will then go on to identify the well documented use of mental health legislation, both historically and in the modern day, as a form of persecution involving the incarceration and drugging of people who were, or are, considered undesirable for one reason or another. And of course the threat of these actions being taken should be considered as being a method of repression in its own right. The use of mental health legislation as form of persecution will also be considered in regard to decomposition methods. Whilst there is an obvious relationship between the two, for one reason or another academics seem reluctant to identify such a form of persecution as a sub-category of decomposition. This seems bizarre to me as from my own experience I can say it is the single biggest factor that prevents a person who knows that they are being targeted by decomposition methods (although they may not know them by this name) from asking others for help and advice.

After giving such background information, my own story is recounted. You may well be surprised at the insidious extent that decomposition methods can reach and be maintained at, for very prolonged periods of time.

A concluding chapter will then sum up my account and where it fits in regard to modern and historical record of decomposition methods. This book is by no means a perfect work but I do sincerely hope that it is a positive step taken in the journey to freedom, both for myself and others. There are reasons why people persecuted in this manner are rarely able to articulate their experiences. I believe I am in a unique situation to be able to do so.

This exposing of decomposition methods comes at a time of increased uncertainty in the world; powerful groups, whether they are intelligence agencies affiliated with a nation-state or not, seek to gain and maintain power through multi-faceted means. Their motivations for the enactment of decomposition methods are their own. It may sound a simple thing to say, but I ask you to remember that just because you would not do something yourself, does not mean that other people think the same way. Among some powerful groups, there is an ambition to exert a controlling and repressive influence over people and decomposition methods are an extreme expression of this. Whether they are rare or not is a different question.

www.ingramcontent.com/pod-product-compliance
Lightning Source LLC
Chambersburg PA
CBHW062114040426
42337CB00042B/2472